ACKNOWLEDGEMENTS

Thanks to Judith Orr, Amy Leather, Mark Thomas, Ian Birchall and
Ken Olende for comments and encouragement, and to Jack Farmer,
Mark Harvey and Peter Robinson for their help in production.

ABOUT THE AUTHOR

Sally Campbell is on the editorial board of *Socialist Review* and is
studying German at Birkbeck College, University of London.

COVER PHOTOGRAPH: Rosa Luxemburg in 1893, while studying in Zurich.

INSIDE FRONT PHOTOGRAPH: Rosa Luxemburg addressing a meeting at
the Stuttgart Congress of the Socialist International, 1907.

INSIDE BACK PHOTOGRAPH: A Spartacist League meeting in Berlin, circa
January 1919.

PUBLISHED BY BOOKMARKS PUBLICATIONS 2011
ISBN 9781905192786
SERIES DESIGNED BY NOEL DOUGLAS (noel@noeldouglas.net)
PRINTED BY MELITA PRESS

A Rebel's Guide to
ROSA LUXEMBURG

SALLY CAMPBELL

★ 1: WHO IS ROSA LUXEMBURG?

Rosa Luxemburg is a much debated figure — even misunderstood and misrepresented. From listening to typical arguments one could conclude that she was a pacifist whose nickname was "Bloody Rosa"; a feminist icon who was not interested in women's liberation; an anti-Leninist who defended the "Red Terror"; a historical determinist who placed absolute faith in the self-activity of workers; and a hard-core, full-time revolutionary who was also a human being.

The one thing everyone agrees on is that her vitality, energy and commitment to everything she did make her an inspiration. She achieved an extraordinary amount in her brutally shortened life, against all the prejudice she faced as a Polish Jew and a woman — and a small one with a limp at that.

Rosa Luxemburg was a revolutionary socialist whose whole life, from her teens in Poland in the 1880s to her murder at the age of 47 in the midst of the German Revolution of 1919, was devoted to bringing about fundamental change.

She was an activist, an orator of great standing, a teacher and a theorist. She threw herself into the struggles developing from the growing workers' movement, as well as stepping back and analysing them. She wrote several key texts, including *The Mass Strike* and *Reform or Revolution*, which developed the Marxist tradition for the new conditions of the 20th century. She was a critical Marxist who insisted on debating strategy in the movement, never assuming someone was right simply because they were older or highly regarded.

She fought to defend the tradition of socialism from below — looking to the self-activity of workers as the foundation of socialism, rather than simply seeking representation in parliament. She recognised the power of the mass strikes that took place in Russia in 1905 and described how they transcended the barriers between political and economic struggles.

She stood, with just a handful of others, against the horror of the First World War while most socialists in Germany and throughout Europe caved in to their own nations' patriotic warmongering. She was imprisoned for much of the war for her principled internationalism against this slaughter which set worker against worker. She found hope and inspiration in the Russian Revolution of 1917.

In this little book I aim to cut through some of the fog surrounding Rosa Luxemburg and restore her to her place as "Red Rosa", the revolutionary. While in such a short space I cannot do her justice, I hope to give a sense of the woman, her ideas and her life, fused as they were with the struggle for the emancipation of all humankind.

★ 2: REBEL CHILD TO REVOLUTIONARY

Rosa Luxemburg was born in March 1871 in Zamosc, a large but declining agricultural town in south eastern Poland. At that time there was no unified Polish state – it was divided between the Russian, German and Austrian empires. Zamosc fell under the rule of the Tsar – Russia's dictator. The town had a thriving Jewish culture – more than a third of the population was Jewish – but the Luxemburg family was very much assimilated into Polish life. Rosa's father, Eliasch, was a timber merchant and the family was moderately well off, though not without spells of hardship.

Rosa was the youngest of five children. When she was a toddler the family moved to Warsaw, also within the Russian Empire, partly because Eliasch wanted the best possible educational opportunities for his children. Soon after, Rosa developed a serious hip disease which kept her bed-ridden for a year and left her with a permanent limp. She used the time well, learning to read and write and composing her first letters to her parents and siblings by the age of five – insisting they formally reply!

For Polish Jews living in the racist and oppressive Russian Empire, getting a good education was not straightforward. Few Poles and no Jews were allowed into the first Warsaw high school, which was reserved for the offspring of Russian officials. There was a strict limit on the number of Jews allowed at the second girls' high school, which Rosa attended. The students were forced to speak Russian — the Polish language was forbidden even outside of classes. This enforced "Russianisation" bred dissent among school students, and Rosa was at the forefront of it. Students rebelled against their teachers and held demonstrations, often in solidarity with struggles taking place in wider Polish society.

There were links between the school students and revolutionary organisations operating in Warsaw, which were largely made up of young intellectuals. Rosa herself, probably by the age of 15, was in contact with these groups. Her activities did not go unnoticed: though she was always top of the class she was denied the gold medal for academic achievement because of her "rebellious attitude toward the authorities" (Paul Frölich, *Rosa Luxemburg*, Pluto, 1972, p25). By the time she was in her final year at school she was almost certainly a member of Proletariat, the first socialist party in Poland.

Proletariat had been inspired by the Narodniks, a Russian revolutionary group which fought to liberate the peasants from the Tsarist autocracy through acts of terrorism — assassinations and bombings. But the Polish group sought to move beyond individual acts by building a mass base among the growing workers' movement in Poland's cities. Poland was more developed industrially than Russia, partly because of its proximity to Western markets and partly because the Tsar was nervous about allowing an industrial working class to develop too near his heartland.

In 1883 Proletariat successfully organised a series of strikes around the country, including a mass strike on the outskirts of Warsaw. The authorities responded with massive repression. Over the next two years many members were arrested and the organisation was effectively destroyed. When Luxemburg was 15, in 1886, four leading members were hanged – the first such public execution in 22 years. Only a few small cells of the organisation survived, and it was one of these that Luxemburg joined. She, like others of her generation, was inspired to take up revolutionary politics by the daily repression meted out by the Tsar's regime. There was no real political freedom in the empire, so becoming an activist committed to the fight for democracy was not an easy path to choose.

The next few years saw a resurgence of workers' struggles and socialist activity in Poland, but this brought new dangers for activists. Luxemburg was forced to go into exile in 1889 to avoid arrest, and opted to go to Switzerland – the destination of choice for Polish socialists. She was smuggled across the border hidden under straw in the back of a cart, having convinced a local priest that she was desperate to convert to Christianity but had to escape her oppressive family in order to do it.

★ 3:
POLAND'S
FREEDOM

Rosa Luxemburg had already been reading the works of Karl Marx and Friedrich Engels since leaving school, and attending university in Zurich (exceptional for a woman at the time) meant that she could undertake intensive study of both capitalist theory and its critics. But exile was not just a study break. In Switzerland, which was full of political émigrés, Luxemburg would meet some of the key figures in Russian and Polish revolutionary politics, not least among them Georgi Plekhanov, the "father of Russian Marxism". She also met Leo Jogiches, a Lithuanian revolutionary recognised as "one of the earliest and most active socialists" in Vilna (Vilnius) (J P Nettl, *Rosa Luxemburg*, abridged edition, Oxford, 1966, p43). They went on to have a personal relationship that lasted many years and a political one that lasted throughout Luxemburg's life.

Luxemburg maintained a close involvement in Polish politics during her time in Switzerland, as did other émigrés. Her confidence as a theorist and as a leader grew as she intervened in debates. In 1892 the fractured left in Poland had pulled itself together into the Polish Socialist Party (PPS), spurred on by an upturn in workers' struggle. But the party's programme was an uneasy mixture of Polish nationalism and Marxism. Luxemburg and her comrades weren't prepared to compromise on their revolutionary internationalism. They argued that Russian workers were their allies against the Tsar who oppressed them all.

This was a rejection of Karl Marx's support for Polish independence, a position he had developed in the 1840s and held until his death in 1883. In his time there was no Russian working class to speak of, so the key division had been between the Polish nation and the Tsar. Luxemburg argued that circumstances had changed with the development of industrial capitalism in Russia. Now an alliance of Polish and Russian workers against the Polish capitalist class and the weak Russian capitalist class, both allied to Tsarism, was possible.

In July 1893 Luxemburg was central to the launch of a new revolutionary socialist paper, *Sprawa Robotnicza* (The Workers' Cause). It was put together by the young exiles in Switzerland led by Luxemburg and her old comrades from Proletariat. The timing of the paper's launch was deliberate. August 1893 was to see the Third Congress of the Socialist International, the conference of all the socialist parties from around the world, which discussed policy, strategy and tactics for the international movement. Launching *Sprawa Robotnicza* would, they hoped, give the group a legitimate claim to be represented at the Congress as part of the Polish delegation so they could argue against the nationalism of the PPS.

The question of independence was important for the Polish movement. This is not surprising given that Poland had been carved up by its neighbours. But while socialists should support the right to self-determination, Rosa Luxemburg argued that the PPS were actually advocating a backward-looking "restoration" of Poland. Luxemburg argued that focusing on an independent Polish state would hinder the fight for liberation for all the oppressed masses living under the Tsar. She attended the Congress, arguing that she should be allowed a mandate to represent this view held by some Polish socialists — even if it was a minority view. The PPS delegation argued hard against her being allowed to speak, but she rose anyway. One attendee, the Belgian socialist leader Emile Vandervelde, recalled the meeting thus:

"Rosa, 23 years old at the time, was quite unknown except in a few socialist circles in Germany and Poland... Her opponents had a great deal of trouble holding their ground against her. I can see her now: how she sprang to her feet out of the sea of delegates and jumped onto a chair to make herself better heard. Small, delicate and dainty in a summer dress which cleverly concealed her physical defects, she advocated her cause with such magnetism in her eyes and with such fiery words that she enthralled and won over the great majority of the congress." (Frölich, pp51-52)

Unfortunately, it was not these delegates who would decide, but a separate commission, which later voted to reject her mandate by nine votes to seven with three abstentions. This was partly because of the influence of Plekhanov, who distrusted the young upstarts from Switzerland — Jogiches and Luxemburg — and backed the PPS.

Luxemburg was furious, but continued to build and argue within the movement. By 1894 she was the editor of *Sprawa Robotnicza*, and the group launched itself as the Social Democratic Party of the Kingdom of Poland (SDKP — a few years later adding "iL" for "and Lithuania"). By the time of the next Congress of the Socialist International in 1896 there was no question of her right to attend and speak on behalf of Polish socialists, despite the smears about the "hysterical female" coming from PPS members.

Still in her twenties, Rosa Luxemburg had fought her way to the front line of Polish socialism. She was the driving force and acknowledged leader of the SDKP, and had made a name for herself in the international movement. She was now ready to move into the most important arena in revolutionary politics at the time: Germany.

★ 4: THE HEART OF THE MOVEMENT

Germany had been a late developer in European capitalism, but in the final quarter of the 19th century it had begun to make up the difference and compete with France and Britain. The dynamic capitalism that Marx and Engels had written about 50 years earlier in the *Communist Manifesto* had been doing its job. People's lives had been transformed from working on the land to being brought together en masse in the giant factories and growing cities of Germany. Communists could now truly talk of "the masses" being their audience.

The most important working class party was the Social Democratic Party of Germany (SPD). The Anti-Socialist Laws brought in by Bismarck in 1878 had lapsed by 1890, so unlike in Russia or Poland socialists were able to organise openly and legally, though there were still some remaining restrictions — a policeman often sat on the platform at SPD public rallies to ensure no laws were broken. The SPD seized the opportunity to throw itself into open recruitment and electioneering. By the late 1890s it had a million members, 4.5 million voters, 90 daily papers around the country, and numerous trade unions and co-operatives (Chris Harman, *The Lost Revolution*, Bookmarks, 1997, p16).

Luxemburg arrived in Berlin in May 1898, having married a friend of a friend, Gustav Lübeck, to gain German citizenship. Though she was an exceptionally confident young woman, it was not easy to make her entrance into the established and bustling metropolis. Soon after arriving she wrote to Leo Jogiches, "I feel as though I have arrived here as a complete stranger and all alone to 'conquer Berlin', and having laid eyes on it, I now feel anxious in the face of its cold power, completely indifferent to me." (*The Letters of Rosa Luxemburg*, Verso, 2011, p40)

But this indifference didn't last long. 1898 was an election year and Luxemburg offered her services to the SPD as a campaigner for the eastern regions of Prussia, which included many Polish-speaking workers. They accepted her offer and she went on a speaking tour which was a triumph. She had absolute theoretical clarity and she took her audience seriously, not just whipping up emotions but putting clear arguments. She returned to Berlin with her confidence restored and a heightened reputation.

She made important political friends in the SPD, among them Karl Kautsky, who was seen as the inheritor of Marx and Engels' legacy. She became close friends with his wife, Luise. She also grew close to Clara Zetkin, who had been involved with the SPD since before it was legal and was editor of the socialist women's paper, *Die Gleichheit* (Equality).

Within a few months of her arrival Luxemburg was to throw herself into a polemic against one of the party's leading theorists in defence of Marx's central argument that the emancipation of the working class must be the act of the working class itself.

★ 5: REFORM OR REVOLUTION?

While formally the SPD was a Marxist party, in practice a split was developing between those who continued to argue for the need for revolution to bring about socialism, and those who increasingly looked to the possibility of reforming the existing state through parliament, rather than overthrowing it. It is worth pointing out that these "reformists" were actually committed to bringing about real change in society and improving workers' lives – unlike the reformists we have known in recent Labour governments, who wholeheartedly accept the idea that "there is no alternative" to privatisation and attacks on the welfare state.

One of the SPD's main theorists was Eduard Bernstein and it was his "revision" of revolutionary Marxism in his 1899 book *The Preconditions of Socialism and the Tasks of Social Democracy* (known in Britain as *Evolutionary Socialism*) which put this argument most clearly.

Bernstein began by claiming that capitalism had changed since Marx's day, a generation before. As capitalism ages, Bernstein argued, it becomes more stable because it "adapts". Monopolies and the credit system could regulate capitalism and rid it of the slumps and crises that Marx identified in *Capital*. So, far from capitalism's contradictions deepening as it aged, they were being alleviated. Capitalism would continue to grow and the task of socialists was to fight for a larger share of the wealth for workers, gradually transforming the unequal system of capitalism into the equal system of socialism.

Luxemburg argued the opposite in what is still one of her best known works, *Reform or Revolution*. While there may be periods of stability, as there had been since 1873, larger units of capital, along with the rising militarism of the great powers, meant greater contradictions and conflicts in the system:

"For him [Bernstein], crises are simply derangements of the economic mechanism. With their cessation, he thinks, the mechanism could function well. But the fact is that crises are not 'derangements' in the usual sense of the word. They are 'derangements' without which capitalist economy could not develop at all... Crises are an organic manifestation inseparable from capitalist economy." (*Reform or Revolution*, Bookmarks, 1989, pp53-54)

Crisis is endemic to capitalism because it is a system based on relentless expansion and competition, and it is the workers and the poor who will be made to pay when those crises break out. The system cannot be tamed; it must be overthrown.

Marx's insight was that capitalism makes the struggle for socialism an economic possibility and a necessity. The means to provide a decent standard of living for everyone now existed, but capitalism could not deliver this – the anarchy of capitalism would bring not progress but destruction. Growth for capitalism meant colonialism, the destruction of cultures and the growing threat of war. So socialism is not just a nice idea, it's necessary for humanity.

Luxemburg quotes Bernstein lamenting this scientific

approach: "Why represent socialism as the consequence of economic compulsion?... Why degrade man's understanding, his feeling for justice, his will?" Luxemburg responded: "Bernstein's superlatively just distribution is to be attained thanks to man's free will, man's will acting not because of economic necessity, since this will itself is only an instrument, but because of man's comprehension of justice, because of man's *idea of justice*... We thus quite happily return to the principle of justice, to the old war horse on which the reformers of the earth have rocked for ages for the lack of surer means of historic transportation. We return to that lamentable Rosinante on which the Don Quixotes of history have galloped towards the great reform of the earth, always to come home with their eyes blackened." (*Reform or Revolution*, pp68-69)

Her point is that the will has always been there, from Spartacus to the Levellers, but never before was an equal distribution of wealth an actual economic possibility. Where Marx had made socialism a science, Bernstein sought to once again make it merely a utopian ideal.

In Germany at this time trade unions and co-operatives were improving the lives of ordinary people, and expanding suffrage would allow more workers' representatives to introduce laws favourable to workers. For Bernstein, this showed that gradually reforming capitalism away was possible. Luxemburg saw trade union struggle and the fight for reforms as crucial, but not a solution in themselves: "The objective conditions of capitalist society transform the two economic functions of the trade unions into a sort of labour of Sisyphus [who, in Greek myth, was condemned to keep rolling a rock up a hill, only for it to roll down again, ad infinitum], which is, nevertheless, indispensable. For as a result of the activity of his trade unions, the worker succeeds in obtaining for himself the rate of wages due to him in accordance with the situation of the labour-power market. As a result of trade union activity, the capitalist law of wages is applied." (*Reform or Revolution*, p67)

Trade unions can win higher wages – by renegotiating the terms of exploitation – and this is important. But they cannot get rid of exploitation altogether. The fight for reforms is necessary training for the fight to overthrow the system – as Tony Cliff pointed out, Sisyphus must have developed very strong muscles – but it is not the same thing.

Bernstein believed socialists could rely on using the state to bring about change, as if it were a neutral tool to be used by whoever is in government. Luxemburg argued that the state is not neutral – it is a class state, representing and working in the interests of the ruling class. She highlighted the nature of the state and its monopoly on violence in the following passage, in a debate with Emile Vandervelde:

"What is actually the whole function of bourgeois legality? If one 'free citizen' is taken by another against his will and confined in close and uncomfortable quarters for a while, everyone understands that an act of violence has been committed. However, as soon as the process takes place in accordance with the book known as the penal code, and the quarters in question refer to the 'Royal Prussian Prison', then it is transformed into an act of peaceful legality. If one man is compelled by another against his will systematically to kill his fellow men, then that is obviously an act of violence. However, as soon as this same process is called 'military service', the good citizen is deluded into believing that he can breathe in the full peace of legality. If one person is deprived against his will of some part of his property or earnings, no one doubts that an act of violence has been committed, but if the process is called 'indirect taxation', then it is merely the exercise of legal rights.

"In other words, what presents itself to us as bourgeois legality is nothing but the violence of the ruling class, a violence raised to an obligatory norm from the outset. Once the individual acts of violence have been raised in this way to an obligatory norm, then the process may be reflected in the mind of the bourgeois jurist (and no less in the mind of the socialist opportunist) not as it really is, but upside down: the 'legal order' appears as an independent creation of abstract 'justice', and the coercive violence of the state as a mere consequence, a mere 'sanctioning' of the law. In reality, the truth is exactly the opposite: bourgeois legality (and parliamentarism as legality in the process of development) is itself only a particular social form expressing the political violence of the bourgeoisie, a violence which has grown up out of the given economic base." (Frölich, p84)

The law is a tool of capitalism; it cannot be a tool for fundamentally transforming the world. Equally "the law" does not prevent violence – it is founded and maintained on violence. To believe that it is possible to use the law to peacefully legislate capitalism away is a fantasy.

So Luxemburg's argument with Bernstein is not that he advocates reforms – this is the essential everyday work of socialists. It is that he sees this as a peaceful, gradual road to socialism, as opposed to the violent path of revolution. But, as Luxemburg puts it, "reform and revolution are not different methods of historic development that can be picked out at pleasure from the counter of history, just as one chooses hot or cold sausages":

"It is contrary to history to represent work for reforms as a long drawn out revolution and revolution as a condensed series of reforms. A social transformation and a legislative reform do not differ according to their duration but according to their content... That is why people who pronounce themselves in favour of the method of legislative reform *in place of and in contradistinction to* the conquest of political power and social revolution, do not really choose a more tranquil, calmer and slower road to the *same* goal, but a *different* goal... Our programme becomes not the realisation of socialism, but the reform of capitalism." (*Reform or Revolution*, pp74-75)

Bernstein counterposes the struggle for reforms and the struggle for revolution; Luxemburg insists on their unity. The fight for reforms is the bridge to revolution.

Luxemburg won a motion at the SPD conference in 1899 committing them to a revolutionary Marxist programme, though this was largely because the heavyweight Kautsky supported her. The success of *Reform or Revolution* gave Rosa Luxemburg a boost in the SPD, but it also won her enemies — not least among trade union bureaucrats who had taken her "labour of Sisyphus" comment very badly. They saw it as a challenge to their position because it highlighted the limits of trade unionism. She spent the next few years engaged in hard debates with various sections of the party, honing her skills in the process. But ensuring the SPD had the correct revolutionary programme was no guarantee. In practice the SPD was moving towards a reformist strategy.

★ 6: THE JOY OF POLEMIC

Luxemburg thrived on living debate, and never held back when she felt an argument was important. In 1899 she attacked the editorial board of the party's main paper, *Vorwärts* (Forward), which she felt was wishy-washy and failed to take a clear revolutionary line. "There are two types of living organisms," she wrote in the smaller paper *Leipziger Volkszeitung* (Leipzig People's Paper), "those who possess a backbone and therefore walk, at times even run; the others, invertebrate, who either creep or cling" (Frölich, p59).

In July 1904 Luxemburg was sentenced to three months' imprisonment for "insulting the Kaiser". In a speech during an election campaign in 1903 she had said of him that, "Any man who talks about the good and secure living of the German workers has no idea of the real facts" (Frölich, p91). She was released early as part of a general amnesty granted to mark the death of the king of Saxony – a fact which annoyed her massively. While in prison at Zwickau she wrote to Karl Kautsky encouraging him to continue their battles in the party after they had successfully passed a motion against revisionism at a congress of the International in Amsterdam:

"And so you have other battles to fight. That makes

me very happy because it shows that those little people feel hard hit by our victory in Amsterdam... Therefore it troubles me that you say you envy my being in a cell! I have no doubt that you will give [our opponents] a good knocking on their so-called heads, but you must do it with joy and relish, not as a burdensome interruption, because the public always senses the mood of the combatants, and if you take pleasure in the fight, it lends a brighter tone to the polemic and gives you a moral advantage... I'm writing all this to you not in order to 'whip you up'...but to make you feel joyful about your polemic." (*Letters*, pp172-173)

Around the same time she engaged in a debate with Russian revolutionary Lenin over party organisation and democracy. In 1902 Lenin had published his famous pamphlet *What is to be Done?* In it Lenin argued that socialists in Russia had to get their act together — while the Russian masses were engaging in strikes and demonstrations, the left was simply tailing them by only talking about immediate economic demands. Instead, socialists must be tightly organised and highly political, studying socialist theory and injecting those ideas into the workers' movement. The party should be primarily made up of professional revolutionaries who would work under the direction of the leadership and be accountable to it, and a party newspaper should be produced centrally which would carry arguments to be applied throughout the movement.

His argument precipitated a split in the Russian socialist movement in 1903, between Lenin's Bolsheviks and the Mensheviks, who wanted a broader, looser party structure. In the conditions of illegality that they faced in Russia, Lenin argued that the broad organisation that the Mensheviks proposed, rather than making the party most accessible to the masses, actually made "revolutionaries most accessible to the police" (*What is to be Done?*). After the split Lenin wrote *One Step Forward, Two Steps Back*, reasserting the need for centralised organisation.

Luxemburg responded in articles in the Russian paper *Iskra* and the German theoretical journal *Neue Zeit* in 1904. She agreed with Lenin on the need for a centralised, disciplined party at the vanguard of the working class movement, but she felt his centralism went too far. For Luxemburg the energy and inventiveness of the living movement was what propelled it forward. Lenin's ultra-centralism was in danger of burying this energy under the strict discipline of the party. As she put it, "Mistakes committed by a genuine revolutionary labour movement are much more fruitful and worthwhile historically than the infallibility of the very best Central Committee."

This wasn't just an argument with Lenin – Luxemburg was also directing her comments at the SPD's leadership, who were thoroughly resistant to any ideas or actions coming up from the movement.

The disagreements between Luxemburg and Lenin have been exaggerated – they respected each other immensely and agreed on the fundamentals of revolutionary politics. Part of the reason for their disagreement over organisation was due to the different circumstances in Germany and Russia – in the former there was a relatively low level of struggle but strong organisation, while in the latter there were feverish strike waves but barely any organisation at all. Luxemburg herself was no stranger to centralised organisation, this being the way the Polish SDKPiL (of which she was the key theoretician until the end of her life) was organised, in conditions of illegality like the Russians.

If Luxemburg thrived on polemic, Lenin lived and breathed it. Between 1902 and 1904 Lenin was waging an argument in the Russian movement, and he "bent the stick" (overstated points in order to convince comrades of a new strategy) as far as necessary in order to pull the movement onto the right path. Just a year later a revolution exploded across Russia and Lenin opened up the party to a much wider membership, changing the structures accordingly. But the centralised nature of the organisation remained, and was to prove invaluable in the struggles to come. The experienced layer of revolutionaries that Lenin nurtured over the next decade was able to give crucial tactical leadership during the Russian Revolution of 1917 in a way that Luxemburg's German Communist Party, only founded in the heat of the German Revolution of 1918, was not.

However, Luxemburg's debate with Lenin was valuable for the movement. It highlighted a fact which cannot be overestimated – that the working class itself, not the revolutionary party, will make the revolution. Luxemburg erred in overestimating the ability of the movement *in itself* to produce the necessary leadership to spearhead the revolution. The question of the relationship between party and class would return within a year, as the spontaneous struggle of the masses took centre stage.

★ 7: 1905: THE FIRST RUSSIAN REVOLUTION

It had long been common sense in the socialist movement that economically and politically backward Russia would be the rearguard of the revolution. The events of 1905 changed that, and in the process transformed all of Europe.

In January 1905 a peaceful demonstration led by a priest, Father Gapon, marched through St Petersburg, the Russian Empire's capital. Some 140,000 people descended on the Winter Palace to hand in a petition to the Tsar demanding a constituent assembly under universal, secret and equal suffrage. Their other demands included universal free education, freedom of the press and of speech, progressive taxation and an eight-hour day. The Tsar's troops were ordered to fire on the protest. They killed hundreds in what became known as "Bloody Sunday".

The massacre immediately opened up a new period of struggle in Russia, with strikes and peasant risings heralding the start of the first Russian Revolution. Most Marxists thought that this was Russia's belated bourgeois-democratic revolution, of the sort that had created the French Republic in 1789. Luxemburg argued that it was much more than this. In her article "The Russian Revolution" (28 January 1905) she argues, "It would be totally wrong-headed if the Social Democracy of Western Europe...were to see in the Russian Revolution merely an historical aping of what Germany and France have already 'gone through' long ago" (Richard B Day and Daniel F Gaido, *Witnesses to Permanent Revolution*, Haymarket, 2011, p358). Precisely because of the time that had passed and the specific class character of Russia this revolution would be a new and unique process.

The French Revolution of 1789 had been led by the liberal petty bourgeoisie — the intelligentsia of the new capitalist class. They had succeeded in uniting capitalists, workers and peasants. The revolution in Russia in 1905 was very different. This democratic revolution was led by the workers and by their intelligentsia — that is, the Social Democrats (Marxists). Luxemburg wrote, "The Russian Revolution has the most pronounced proletarian class character of all revolutions to date."

Within two weeks of Bloody Sunday the revolution had spread to all major cities across the Russian Empire, from Poland to the Ukraine to the Baltic states. Luxemburg argued for the necessity of maintaining "the revolutionary situation in permanence". The decisive factor was leadership — who could agitate, educate and encourage the class to carry the struggle further? For Luxemburg the answer was clear: "This task can *only* be fulfilled in Russia by Social Democracy, which rises above every particular moment of the struggle because it has a final aim that goes beyond all particular moments; which for that reason does not see the end of the world in the immediate success or failure of the moment; and for whom the working class is not a means to the end of achieving political freedom, but political freedom is rather a means to the end of emancipating the working class" (Day and Gaido, p371).

The revolution did begin to develop in the way Luxemburg hoped. Strikes became mass strikes, involving thousands of workers and raising the question of who runs society. Political strikes spread and became economic strikes over pay and conditions, which in turn fed into larger political strikes.

Russia was no longer the backward rump of the movement, but the vanguard of workers' activity.

In December 1905 Luxemburg smuggled herself into revolutionary Poland to experience the struggle first hand. Having made it to Warsaw, she immediately set to work. She fought to produce newspapers to intervene in and direct the struggle. Some reforms had been won in the autumn, including the Tsar conceding a duma (parliament) with limited suffrage. In December the revolution reached its climax with a workers' uprising in Moscow that lasted eight days. But the rising was isolated and overcome by the Tsar's troops, and the revolutionary wave receded.

Within three months of arriving in Warsaw Luxemburg was arrested and she was imprisoned for four months. She was expelled from Warsaw after her release and went to Finland, where she determined to analyse the most exciting year of her life.

★ 8: LEARNING THE LESSONS OF THE MASS STRIKE

The events in Russia inspired workers in Germany to wage their own battles. In the years 1900 to 1904 there were 477,516 workers involved in strikes or lockouts in Germany. In 1905 alone 507,964 workers were involved in strikes — more than in any other single year from 1848 to 1917 (Carl E Schorske, *Social Democracy in Germany, 1905-1917*, Harvard, 1955, p31).

In January 1905 coal miners in the industrial Ruhr district of Germany went on strike over their dreadful working conditions. But this strike was different: it spread like wildfire from organised to unorganised workers, bypassing the attempts of union leaders to keep it within strict limits. The strike was called off after a month, but it left behind a simmering political demand on the local authorities to intervene to improve working conditions. The strike had gone from economic demands on the bosses to political demands on parliamentary representatives. What's more, this struggle had been led by the

workers themselves, despite their leaders – the spontaneous outpouring of bitterness had been the driving force.
As Luxemburg said, the party and the trade unions had a
choice between "placing itself at the head of the flood or
being swept aside by it" (Schorske, p38).

A gap was developing between the reformist trade
union bureaucracy, which was worried about how much
all the strikes were costing and whether it could control
them, and the rank and file membership of the unions,
which increasingly looked to radical politics for a lead. The
SPD, meanwhile, tended to separate the struggle into the
"two pillars" of the trade unions (economic struggle) and
the party (political struggle), and so didn't seek to lead the
striking workers. This reformist approach of separating
"political" from "economic" struggle endures today, with
successive Labour Party leaders refusing to back strikes
for fear of damaging their "electability".

Luxemburg wrote a pamphlet called *The Mass Strike,
the Political Party and the Trade Unions* in 1906 in order
to wage an argument inside the SPD about the lessons of
the 1905 Russian Revolution. She describes the impact
of the movement in Russia: "For the first time [it] awoke
feeling and class consciousness in millions upon millions
as if by an electric shock... The proletarian mass...quite
suddenly and sharply came to realise how intolerable
was that social and economic existence which they had
patiently endured for decades in the chains of capitalism.
Thereupon there began a spontaneous general shaking of
and tugging at these chains." (*The Mass Strike*, Bookmarks,
2005, p33)

Luxemburg's analysis is a key insight into revolution in
the mass age – something Marx could not have witnessed

50 years earlier, though the *Communist Manifesto* points towards it. Luxemburg understood and gave theoretical form to the movement of the modern worker: "The mass strike is the first natural, impulsive form of every great revolutionary struggle of the proletariat." This has been vindicated many times since — in Russia in 1917, Germany in 1918-23, Italy in 1920, Hungary in 1956, France in 1936 and again in 1968, Iran in 1978-79, Poland in 1980 and Egypt in 2011.

Luxemburg confronted the "two pillars" approach of her party leaders and the trade unions:

"But the movement on the whole does not only go in one direction, from the economic to the political struggle, but also in the opposite direction... Every new onset and every fresh victory of the political struggle is transformed into a powerful impetus for the economic struggle... After every foaming wave of political action a fertile sediment remains, from which a thousand stalks of economic struggle shoot forth...

"In a word: the economic struggle is the transmitter from one political centre to another; the political struggle is the periodic fertilisation of the soil for the economic struggle. Cause and effect here continually change places; and thus the economic and the political factors in the period of the mass strike, now widely removed, completely separated or even mutually exclusive, as the theoretical plan would have them, merely form the two interlacing sides of the proletarian class struggle." (*The Mass Strike*, pp50-51)

Think of the revolution in Egypt that began in January 2011. The mass demonstrations which erupted in Cairo didn't come from nowhere, but were the culmination of a decade of struggles, both political and economic. Political struggles for democratic rights and against imperialism combined with the pressures of the global economic crisis to bring about a mass movement. But it wasn't until the protesters in Tahrir Square were bolstered by a general strike across Egypt that they were able to topple dictator Hosni Mubarak and begin to change Egypt fundamentally.

Luxemburg sought to illuminate how mass strikes could become revolutionary, not on the command of a party, but through the revolutionary instincts of the class itself. The job of the party was to give direction to those struggles.

The SPD was in danger of failing this test. At the Jena congress in September 1905 the party voted to support mass strikes only in the most limited of circumstances, when they could be used to defend powers won by the electoral strategy. A year later Eduard David, a leading revisionist in the SPD, said, "The brief May flowering of the new revolutionism is happily over. The party will again devote itself with undivided heart to the positive exploitation and expansion of its parliamentary power." (Schorske, p53) For the revisionists the mass strike was an undirected blip which they hoped would quickly disappear so things could "return to normality". For Luxemburg it was both a spontaneous expression of mass working class consciousness and a principal policy of the Social Democrats.

The rest of Luxemburg's life was defined by her absolute faith in the potential for workers' self-emancipation. Her profound understanding of the ebb and flow of workers' struggle expressed in *The Mass Strike* makes her one of the most important contributors to Marxism in the 20th century.

★ 9: NATIONALISM REARS ITS HEAD

In the late 19th century the European powers Britain, France, Italy, Belgium, Germany and Portugal had grabbed territories to rule and exploit, in what became known as the Scramble for Africa. This vicious race meant the subjugation of millions of people and increased tensions between the European empires.

The German state was only unified in 1871 and the Kaiser held relatively few territories in Africa. But competition between the rival industrial powers meant the ruling class was keen to cultivate nationalist feeling. Dozens of nationalist organisations had sprung up, such as the Navy League and the Pan-German League. Some had mass memberships and together they could claim over 1.5 million members (David Blackbourn, *The Fontana History of Germany, 1780-1918*, Fontana, 1997, p428).

Chancellor Bernhard von Bülow, head of the government from 1900 to 1909, was an avowed imperialist and wanted to strengthen and expand Germany's empire, but this was threatened by a popular revolt in German South West Africa in 1904 which was followed by several years of unrest. In the Reichstag the mainstream Centre Party joined together with the opposition parties including the SPD to refuse Bülow's request for compensation for white settlers and then also his request for 29 million marks to put down the rebellion militarily.

Bülow responded by dissolving parliament and "taking the matter to the people" in 1907, declaring, "What is at stake is our whole national political position and more than that, our position in the world." (William Carr, *A History of Germany, 1815-1945*, Hodder, 1972, p187) He employed the energies of the members of the nationalist leagues, who held mass rallies, produced pamphlets and leaflets, and whipped up nationalism. Bülow denounced the SPD as anti-German enemies within and tarred any parties that worked with them by association. His strategy apparently worked. Bülow emerged from the election strengthened, and although the SPD's vote went up, their allocation of seats fell from 81 to 43. This was largely down to run-off second ballots in seats where there was no clear majority — the other parties combined to keep the socialists out, having succumbed to the red-baiting.

The result left the SPD internally divided. The revisionists drew the conclusion that they had lost because they were too radical. Kautsky, speaking for the left wing of the SPD, argued that the result was simply a sign that the class struggle was intensifying. They could not rely on the middle classes to keep voting for them and must focus on building among the working class.

This division had already reared its head at the SPD's congress in Mannheim a few months earlier in 1906. Karl Liebknecht, a leading radical in the party, had proposed an anti-militarist motion which was immediately shot down by party leader August Bebel. Then another delegation submitted a proposal which argued that, if the German government sent troops to help crush the Russian

Revolution, the SPD and the trade unions should call a mass strike to prevent it. Bebel argued that if Germany did go to war against Russia then the nationalistic fever would be so great, and the German masses so caught up in it, that there would be nothing the SPD could do to influence them. The radicals, including Luxemburg, were shocked by this statement. Where was the revolutionary internationalism that had characterised Marxism since its inception? Bebel was arguing they should abandon their revolutionary brothers and sisters in Russia to their fate and he was absolving the SPD of any obligation to fight for the leadership of the working class at home.

The logic of Bebel's arguments went further in the parliamentary debates leading to the 1907 election. Rather than condemning colonialism as a brutal policy and speaking against militarism at home and abroad, Bebel argued that botched colonialism took valuable resources away from the German army, impairing its ability to fight as proudly as it had done in the past. Another SPD deputy, Gustav Noske, backed Bebel, saying that the SPD would defend Germany against attack "with as much determination as any gentleman on the right side of the House" (Schorske, p77).

Later that year, at the Stuttgart Congress of the International, the debates continued. Bebel and the German delegation argued to keep anti-militarism off the agenda as a lost cause. Luxemburg was attending as a representative of the Polish party, and she spoke forcefully on behalf of both the Polish and the Russian delegations to defend revolutionary internationalism. She won an amendment stating, "In the case of the threat of an outbreak of war, it is the duty of the working classes and their parliamentary representatives in the countries taking part...to do everything to prevent the outbreak of war by whatever means seem to them most effective... Should war break out in spite of all this, it is their duty to intercede for its speedy end, and to strive with all their power to make use of the violent economic and political crisis brought about by the war to rouse the people, and thereby to hasten the abolition of capitalist class rule." (Nettl, p270)

The debates were a sign of things to come. Luxemburg, Liebknecht and the handful of others who dared to speak out against Bebel's nationalism would go on to do exactly what the resolution above stated — turn war into revolution. Noske, on the other hand, would go on to play a despicable role in crushing the revolution.

★ 10: KAUTSKY AND THE MARXIST CENTRE

In her speech at the Stuttgart Congress Luxemburg had renewed her war on the revisionists in the SPD, but by 1910 another, more personally painful division became clear in the party.

In spring 1910 a series of mass protests broke out in Germany for electoral reform, and they coincided with big strikes by miners and building workers. For the first time since 1905 the working class was showing signs of going on the offensive. Luxemburg argued for the SPD to give a lead to these struggles, using the tactic of the political mass strike as its weapon. Either the movement must intensify, or it was at risk of petering out. She wrote an article for *Neue Zeit* outlining her position — but Karl Kautsky, its editor, refused to publish it.

Kautsky had been Luxemburg's friend and comrade since she first arrived in Berlin. Politically they had been close and were considered the leading members of the radical wing of the party. Now he seemed to do a complete turnaround. Not only did he reject her article but he wrote a stinging attack on her position, arguing that there was no possibility of the current strikes developing into anything, and that they must wait for the next election in two years. It seemed he no longer saw revolution as sprouting from the self-activity of the workers, as Marx had argued, but instead from the election successes of the SPD.

Kautsky from then on took every opportunity to attack Luxemburg for her "rebel's impatience", but he also continued to attack the revisionists in the party for their willingness to collaborate with the bourgeois parties. So the party now effectively had three currents: the revisionists led by Bernstein; the "Marxist Centre" led by Kautsky, whose fine words justified a collapse into reformism in practice; and the left Radicals led by Luxemburg, Liebknecht, Zetkin and a handful of others.

In 1911 the Morocco Crisis deepened the divisions in the party. In July the German navy sailed a warship into the port of Agadir, claiming they needed to protect German interests in Morocco. This provoked a major diplomatic crisis and strengthened the hand of those in France and Germany pushing for war. The Socialist International wanted to call a meeting to discuss putting out a statement against Germany's actions, but they received a letter from the SPD leadership saying this wasn't necessary — it was best not to risk provoking anti-socialist feeling so close to an election.

Anti-war protests had begun to erupt in Berlin and other parts of Germany and were enthusiastically supported by Luxemburg and her comrades, but the SPD leadership failed to respond in any way. In exasperation Luxemburg published the letter, exposing the SPD leaders for their inaction in the face of growing imperialism.

From the Morocco Crisis onwards the fight against imperialism and war became the key issue shaping debates in the party. Three positions emerged. The revisionists clung to the idea that the cause of socialism could best be served by supporting the German state, and thus gaining reforms through parliament. The SPD deputies of this wing spent their time lobbying for better conditions and weapons for German soldiers. Kautsky and the Centre argued that an anti-imperialist alliance could be formed with industrial capitalists, who (apart from arms manufacturers) had nothing to gain from the arms race and the threat of war. Germany and Britain, he argued, would be much better off coming to an agreement rather than threatening their profits through war. The Centre was advocating disarmament on the basis of its benefits for capitalism. For Luxemburg and the Radicals a capitalist peace was no peace at all but merely contained the seeds of the next war – the great European empires were rubbing against each other and whipping up their own populations into nationalistic fervour. The task for revolutionaries was to counter this with internationalism and mass struggles – to turn the imperialist crisis into a revolutionary movement. Kautsky's position won the day in the SPD in the course of 1912-13.

★ 11:
THEORISING
IMPERIALISM

Throughout these years of fierce debate in the party Luxemburg had been developing her own understanding of capitalism and its relation to colonialism, empire and war. From 1907 onwards she had been employed as a teacher at the SPD's Party School in Berlin. She taught economics with an enthusiasm and clarity that delighted her students, mostly workers ranging in age from 20 to 40-something. She began writing (though never finished) a book called *Introduction to Political Economy*, in which she looked at pre-capitalist, communal forms of society — what Marx had described as "primitive communism" — some examples of which still existed at the time. She showed how this egalitarian way of life characterised by the common ownership of the means of production had been the dominant form of organisation for human societies for millennia. She also powerfully described how capitalist imperialism was destroying such societies:

"The intrusion of European civilisation was a disaster in every sense for primitive social relations. The European conquerors are the first who are not merely after subjugation and economic exploitation, but the means of production itself, by ripping the land from underneath the feet of the native population. In this way, European capitalism deprives the primitive social order of its foundation. What emerges is something that is worse than all oppression and exploitation, total anarchy and

a specifically European phenomenon, the uncertainty of
social existence. The subjugated peoples, separated from
their means of production, are regarded by European
capitalism as mere labourers, and when they are useful
for this end they are made into slaves, and if they are
not, they are exterminated." (Peter Hudis and Kevin B
Anderson (eds), *The Rosa Luxemburg Reader*, Monthly
Review Press, 2004, pp16-17)

But what was it that drove capitalists to expand
and conquer in this way? Luxemburg felt that Marx had
not adequately accounted for this – after all, the age of
imperialism had come after his death. Her major work,
The Accumulation of Capital (1913), attempted to explain
the drive to imperialism.

Luxemburg identified what she felt was a flaw in
Volume 2 of Marx's *Capital*. For Marx accumulation was a
central feature of capitalism. It means simply that capitalists, rather than consuming their profits as luxury goods,
reinvest some of their surplus into capital – either in the
form of new plant or machinery or in hiring more workers –
thus expanding production. This expansion is, in principle,
limitless, and is driven by competition between capitalists.

Luxemburg argued that it was impossible for production to expand "in a society in which there are only
capitalists and workers", as in Marx's model in *Capital*.
Workers, by definition the exploited class, wouldn't have
enough wages to buy the expanded amount of goods.
There would be a crisis of underconsumption and the
capitalists would have to look abroad to non-capitalist
markets to realise their profits. In doing this they would
effectively export capitalism, import cheap raw materials
and increase the stability of the imperialist power at home.

So for Luxemburg imperialist expansion into non-capitalist areas is necessary to capitalist accumulation, but also destroys those areas and absorbs them into capitalism. Thus, in reality, there are very real, physical limits to expansion. Once it absorbs all non-capitalist areas, capitalism must collapse into terminal crisis.

Other Marxists have since criticised her approach, arguing that she took Marx's abstract model in *Capital* Volume 2 too literally, and that Marx's description of accumulation points out that capitalists rely on the consumption of their goods by other capitalists — for example by selling machinery to each other — as much as on the sale of consumer goods to workers. Central to Marx's theory of crisis is the tendency for the rate of profit to fall as accumulation increases, rather than underconsumption. (I have only summarised here, for further reading see the end of this book.)

There have also been more influential Marxist studies of imperialism. The classic work is Nikolai Bukharin's *Imperialism and World Economy*, which shows how imperialism is tied up with the concentration and centralisation of capital as it ages. This both increases the links between capital and the nation-state and drives the expansion of capital overseas.

What Bukharin and Luxemburg have in common is an insistence that imperialism is no blip on the smooth face of capitalism, or a mistaken policy by a particular party. Imperialism is absolutely intrinsic to the system and cannot be understood separately from it. Kautsky's attempts to reform away militarism were doomed to fail. The fight against war and imperialism is central to the fight against capitalism.

★ 12: THE COUNTDOWN TO WAR

Rosa Luxemburg did not let the party's backing of Kautsky hold her back in the fight against war. In December 1913 she founded a new paper, *Sozialdemokratische Korrespondenz* (Social Democratic Correspondence), along with two other Radicals, Franz Mehring and Julian Marchlewski-Karski.

They used it to intervene in the debates in the party and to spread their anti-war views. Luxemburg's articles and campaigning soon put her in the sights of the authorities. On 20 February 1914 she was arrested for inciting soldiers to mutiny. The charge referred back to a speech she had made in September 1913 when she'd said, "If they expect us to lift the weapons of murder against our French or other foreign brothers, then let us tell them 'No, we won't do it!'" At her trial she made a further speech, denouncing militarism and laying out the revolutionary position on war. The prosecutor demanded imprisonment for one year and immediate arrest, to which Luxemburg responded:

"Just a word on the outrageous attack made on me, an attack which recoils on its originator. The Public Prosecutor said — and I have noted his exact words — that he is asking for my immediate arrest because 'it would be incomprehensible if the accused did not take to flight'. In other words, he was saying: 'If I, the Public Prosecutor, had to serve a year in prison, then I would try to escape'. Sir, I believe you; you would run away. A social democrat does not; he stands by his deeds and laughs at your punishments. And now, sentence me." (Frölich, p186)

She was sentenced to a year but was not arrested immediately, and went straight out on a speaking tour of many mass meetings, filled with workers enraged at her harsh sentence. She was able to keep operating for months while her appeal went through its laborious process, and it wasn't until 1915 that she was actually incarcerated. In the meantime the class struggle was sharpening and anti-war feeling was growing. Luxemburg gained a new lease of life. Her agitation for mass strikes against war was getting a hearing — workers were flocking to her meetings. Her words had never before had such a resonance. But the new hope that Luxemburg felt was about to be suddenly and shockingly extinguished.

Even after the assassination of Austro-Hungarian crown prince Franz Ferdinand by Serbian nationalists in June 1914, anti-war activity was rife. Luxemburg and the SPD organised mass rallies and the SPD headquarters put out statements confirming their stance against war right up until the end of July: "The class-conscious proletariat of Germany, in the name of humanity and civilisation, raises a flaming protest against this criminal activity of the warmongers." But at the start of August war was declared and the International crumbled. First Austria declared war on Serbia, and Austrian socialist Adler spoke of their utter helplessness in the face of such nationalist fervour. Then Russia declared against Austria and Germany declared against Russia. While the Bolsheviks and some smaller socialist parties in Serbia, Bulgaria and Poland held firm against the imperialist war, the SPD deputies in the Reichstag voted for the war credits on 4 August. In the SPD's pre-vote discussions only 15 out of 111 deputies had opposed the war, including Karl Liebknecht, but they were refused permission to register a minority position, and agreed not to break party discipline.

The SPD's actions had a terrible impact on socialists everywhere – it was after all the biggest, strongest, most organised party of the International – the inheritor of Marx and Engels' legacy. They had betrayed everything they had claimed to stand for, and without them, the International meant nothing. Lenin at first refused to believe what he was told had happened; Rosa Luxemburg was shattered. But she quickly regained her sense of what had to be done, and that very evening she held a meeting in her flat in Berlin with a handful of revolutionaries including Mehring and Karski, and with support from Clara Zetkin in Stuttgart, and they agreed to take up the struggle against war and against their own party. In December 1914 Liebknecht voted against further war credits and joined them. This was the beginning of the group that was to become Spartacus.

Kautsky did theoretical somersaults to justify the party's stance, claiming this war was "different" from other wars. He made light of the collapse of the International, claiming, "It is not an effective weapon in wartime; it is essentially an instrument of peace." (Frölich, p214) In so saying, he condemned millions of workers to be sent off to slaughter each other, with a pat on the back from the SPD. Lenin saw for the first time what Kautsky had become: "Rosa Luxemburg was right; she realised long ago that Kautsky was a time-serving theorist, serving the majority of the party, serving opportunism in short. There is nothing in the world more pernicious and dangerous for the intellectual independence of the proletariat than the horrid self-satisfaction and base hypocrisy of Kautsky, who glosses over everything and attempts to lull the awakening conscience of the workers with sophistry and pseudo-scientific verbosity." (Frölich, p217)

Luxemburg's group founded a new paper, *Die Internationale*, in January 1915. In its first (and what turned out to be only) issue Luxemburg laid into Kautsky: "In Kautsky's rendering, the world-historical appeal of the *Communist Manifesto* has been subjected to a substantial amendment, and now reads: 'Proletarians of all countries, unite in peacetime, but slit one another's throats in war!'" (Frölich, p218)

★ 13: RESISTANCE IN WARTIME

Rosa Luxemburg was imprisoned in February 1915. Her health was bad and she had been preparing to go away when she was suddenly snatched and taken to a women's prison in Berlin. She was to remain incarcerated with only brief spells of freedom for almost the whole of the war. She hadn't been particularly dreading being locked up – she'd handled it before. But this time she knew just how badly her leadership was needed on the outside. Her group was working with some members of the Marxist Centre who were not prepared to go as far as Kautsky in justifying the war, but there was no fire in the opposition movement.

Luxemburg wrote a pamphlet called *The Crisis of Social Democracy* and smuggled it out by April 1915. It was later published and distributed illegally under the pseudonym Junius and is known as the *Junius Pamphlet*. In it she describes the horrors of war: "Shamed, dishonoured, wading in blood and dripping with filth, thus capitalist society stands. Not as we usually see it, playing the roles of peace and righteousness, of order, of philosophy, of ethics – but as a roaring beast, as an orgy of anarchy, as a pestilential breath, devastating culture and humanity – so it appears in all its hideous nakedness." (Hudis and Anderson, p313)

The *Junius Pamphlet* was also a fierce attack on the SPD for its failure to put out a call to revolutionaries and to the working class movement. This was not a moment to be quiet or to wait for the war to end – this was a cross-roads for humanity: "Either the triumph of imperialism and the destruction of all culture, and, as in ancient Rome, depopulation, desolation, degeneration, a vast cemetery; or, the victory of socialism, that is, the conscious struggle of the international proletariat against imperialism, against its methods, against war. This is the dilemma of world history, its inevitable choice, whose scales are trembling in the balance, awaiting the decision of the proletariat." (Hudis and Anderson, p321)

This either-or – socialism or barbarism – is perhaps Luxemburg's most famous pronouncement. It gets to the heart of her political approach and speaks to us today in a world faced with climate change and nuclear weapons. Revolutionary Marxism is not deterministic, but rather puts the conscious action of people at the centre of everything. People's choices, not "History", will determine the future:

"This madness will not stop, and this bloody nightmare of hell will not cease until the workers of Germany, of France, of Russia and of England will wake up out of their drunken sleep, will clasp each other's hands in brother-hood and will drown the bestial chorus of war agitators and the hoarse cry of capitalist hyenas with the mighty cry of labour, 'Proletarians of all countries, unite!'" (Hudis and Anderson, p341)

By the end of 1915 this call had some resonance – the bodies were piling up and hopes of a quick victory were fading. In December, 20 SPD deputies finally joined Liebknecht in voting against new war credits. As one SPD member wrote, "The masses are restive about the war and especially over the rising cost of living." (Nettl, p390) Luxemburg was released in February 1916 to be met by a thousand women supporters who brought her gifts and shook her hand. She immediately got to work alongside Liebknecht, organising and agitating.

At the May Day demonstration in Berlin on 1 May 1916 Liebknecht made a fiery speech, ending with the words, "Down with the war! Down with the government!" He was immediately arrested and taken to prison to await trial. This proved to be a turning point. On his arrest thousands protested. At the start of his trial mass demonstrations took place in Berlin and when he was sentenced to two and a half years hard labour (later increased to four years by a military court) 55,000 munitions workers went on strike, organised by the Revolutionary Shop Stewards, a network of industrial militants. The workers of Germany were beginning to awaken.

★ 14: REVOLUTION IN RUSSIA

The impact of war was far greater in Russia than in the other nations. Shortages and terrible working conditions led to strikes at the start of 1917. They soon spread, and in the course of the strikes workers resurrected the soviets, or workers' councils, first seen in the 1905 Revolution. Within a week the hated Tsar abdicated and a provisional government was set up, promising universal suffrage.

Rosa Luxemburg had been thrown back in prison without trial in July 1916, but she followed events as closely as she could, though she had to rely on newspapers which had been instructed by the authorities that "all that explains or praises the proceedings of the revolutionaries in Russia must be suppressed" (Nettl, p420). She welcomed the revolution, writing for *Spartacus* in May 1917, "For three years Europe has been like a musty room, almost suffocating those living in it. Now all at once a window has been flung open, a fresh, invigorating gust of air is blowing in, and everyone in the room is breathing deeply and freely of it."

But she also understood that the working class in backward Russia could not win alone: "There is only one serious guarantee against these natural concerns for the future of the Russian Revolution: the awakening of the German proletariat, the attainment of a position of power by the German 'workers and soldiers' in their own country, a revolutionary struggle for peace by the German people... With the German 'workers and soldiers', peace would be concluded immediately and would rest upon solid foundations.

"Thus the question of peace is in reality bound up with the unimpeded, radical development of the Russian Revolution. But the latter is in turn bound up with the parallel revolutionary struggles for peace on the part of the French, English, Italian and, especially, the German proletariat." (http://marxists.org/archive/luxemburg/1917/04/oldmole.htm)

The Russian Revolution did develop in the course of 1917, with the workers' councils challenging the rule of the provisional government and strikes and demonstrations exploding through the summer. In October the Bolsheviks led an insurrection with the slogan "All power to the soviets" and the provisional government fell.

Luxemburg wrote to Clara Zetkin from prison, "The events in Russia are of amazing grandeur and tragedy. Lenin and his people will not of course be able to win out against the insuperable tangle of chaos, but their attempt, by itself, stands as a deed of world-historical significance and a genuine milestone." (*Letters*, p447) She was depressed at the lack of response by German workers and, crucially, their "leadership" in the SPD. She strongly rejected the argument, put by Kautsky and many others since, that the revolution was "premature", that Russia was too backward for socialist revolution – for her the key was to spread the revolution to Germany.

She wrote to Luise Kautsky, "Are you happy about

the Russians? Of course they won't be able to survive this Witches' Sabbath – not because statistics show such backward economic development in Russia, as your clever spouse has it all worked out, but because the Social Democracy in the highly developed West consists of miserable cowardly dogs, who, while looking on calmly, will let the Russians bleed to death. But a downfall like that is better than 'living on for the Fatherland'. It is a world-historical deed, the traces of which will not have disappeared eons from now." (*Letters*, p452)

She saw it as her duty to analyse the events in Russia and learn the lessons as they emerged. In September 1918 she wrote a pamphlet, *The Russian Revolution*, which criticised the Bolsheviks for a lack of democracy that she thought would lead to trouble in the future. It was never finished and was not published in her lifetime, but it has since been used as ammunition against Lenin and further evidence of a gulf between Luxemburg and Bolshevism. In fact, she praised the Bolsheviks for their role: "The party of Lenin was the only one which grasped the mandate and duty of a truly revolutionary party... Only a party which knows how to lead, that is to advance things, wins support in stormy times." (Hudis and Anderson, p289)

However, she did have four specific areas of criticism: the land question, the national question, the constituent assembly and political freedom.

She argued that the Bolsheviks' policy of calling on the peasants to seize the land and divide it up between themselves, rather than nationalising the land, would create problems by strengthening private property. It did indeed cause trouble, but the Bolsheviks had no real alternative. In order to win the revolution with such a small working

class they had to get the peasants on side. Without this policy there would have been no revolution to debate. The Bolsheviks' policy was also far more democratic than the forced nationalisation that Luxemburg proposed.

She also criticised their slogan of self-determination for all the peoples of the Russian Empire. Luxemburg thought that instead they should have called for revolutionary unity of the empire under soviet control. But Lenin understood that forcing the Eastern peoples, who had been oppressed by the Tsar, to accede to soviet power would only drive them away into nationalism. The best way to ensure maximum unity was to offer genuine self-determination which would then bring revolutionary support in return – again, a much more democratic position. Luxemburg's abstract internationalism here would have been disastrous.

Luxemburg pointed out that the Bolsheviks had called for a constituent assembly only to abolish it once they were in power. She proposed joint rule by the soviets and constituent assembly. But for the Bolsheviks the soviets were the *highest* form of democracy – they were bodies formed of workers' delegates, democratically elected and more sensitive to the moods of the masses and shifting needs of the struggle. The constituent assembly represented bourgeois democracy, a limited form of democracy that leaves untouched the power of the capitalists over the economy. Luxemburg came to understand this just two months later when she was in the thick of her own revolution in November 1918: "To resort to the National Assembly today is consciously or unconsciously to turn the revolution back to the historical stage of bourgeois revolutions; anyone advocating it is a secret agent of the bourgeoisie or an unconscious spokesman of petit-bourgeois ideology... Today it is not a question of democracy or dictatorship. The question that history has placed on the agenda is: bourgeois democracy or socialist democracy? For the dictatorship of the proletariat is democracy in a socialist sense." (www. marxists.org/archive/luxemburg/1918/11/20.htm)

At the heart of Luxemburg's criticism was her belief in the self-emancipation of the working class. As the new soviet state was forced to cede huge amounts of land, including key industries and resources, to German imperialism after the treaty of Brest-Litovsk and the civil war began, Luxemburg feared that the levels of centralisation the Bolsheviks were being driven to would impede democracy and lead to a dictatorship, not of the proletariat, but of the party. However, she understood the external limitations on Lenin and the Bolsheviks: "Everything that happens in Russia is comprehensible and represents an inevitable chain of causes and effects, the starting point and end term of which are the failure of the German proletariat and the occupation of Russia by German imperialism. It would be demanding something superhuman from Lenin and his comrades if we should expect from them that under such circumstances they should conjure forth the finest democracy, the most exemplary dictatorship of the proletariat, and a flourishing socialist economy. By their determined revolutionary stand, their exemplary strength in action and their unbreakable loyalty to international socialism, they have contributed whatever could possibly be contributed under such devilishly hard conditions." (Hudis and Anderson, p309)

The key to resolving the Russian Revolution's problems lay in spreading the struggle abroad.

★ 15: REVOLUTION IN GERMANY

In October and November of 1918 the war was going badly for Germany, but the generals refused to accept it. Political strikes against the war began sweeping through munitions factories, followed by mutiny at the naval base at Kiel. The government didn't know how to respond, and the mutiny spread. Soldiers' councils sprang up at the front and workers' councils soon followed around the country. The German Revolution had begun.

The old ruling class were not willing to let go of power easily – and they knew how to hold on to it. Throughout the war the SPD had cooperated with the ruling parties and done their bidding in the name of national unity – now the ruling class hoped the SPD could save them. The leader of the SPD was Friedrich Ebert. He had told the chancellor, Prince Max, "Unless the Kaiser abdicates, a revolution is inevitable. But I will have none of it. I hate it like sin." (Harman, p42) On 9 November a general strike brought the revolution to Berlin. Prince Max handed over the chancellorship to Ebert in the hope that this would calm the revolution. The monarchy fled and a German Republic was declared by SPD member Scheidemann. Just a few streets away Liebknecht was declaring a socialist republic.

This was the central problem with the German Revolution. The SPD – still a workers' party, still committed in word to socialism — was co-opted into government in order to limit the revolution. Yet it was still able to hold sway over the majority of workers and claim to be on their side. During the war the Centre faction had split from the SPD and formed the Independent SPD, which the Spartacus group had joined. In reality the Independents were divided and the Spartacus group was weak and small. So even as Luxemburg — now freed from prison by the revolution — and Liebknecht were agitating for genuine socialist revolution, Ebert was forming a "revolutionary socialist government" made up of SPD and Independent SPD representatives. Their express purpose — agreed with the German military General Staff — was to suppress the revolution by force.

Nonetheless, for a few weeks there was a situation of "dual-power" when both the workers' councils and Ebert's government were running Germany. The Spartacists launched a new paper, *Rote Fahne* (Red Flag), on 18 November. Luxemburg's article clearly warned of Ebert's aims: "The current government is calling a constituent assembly in order to create a bourgeois counterweight to the Workers' and Soldiers' Councils, thereby shunting the revolution onto the track of a mere bourgeois revolution and conjuring away its socialist aims." (Frölich, p271) But Luxemburg and the revolutionaries had no counterweight of their own — no serious organisation capable of leading the revolution beyond a republic.

In December 1918 the Spartacus group convened a conference to found the German Communist Party. They were joined by a group called the Left Radicals and by other young activists from around Germany who had been swept up in the revolution. Weaknesses were apparent straight away. One of the first questions to be debated was whether to stand in the elections for the National Assembly. While the Communists opposed the assembly in principle, Luxemburg argued that they must participate in order to denounce the chamber for what it was: "In order to mobilise the masses *against* the National Assembly and appeal to them to wage a very intensive struggle against it, we must utilise the elections and the platform of the National Assembly itself." (Frölich, p285) All the other leading members agreed with her, but the younger membership, convinced that the revolution was soon to win, couldn't see the point of participating in elections they opposed. The motion was lost, and it was a sign to Rosa Luxemburg that she must warn against impatience and impetuous action.

★ 16:
COUNTER-
REVOLUTION

On 7 December Liebknecht had been seized at his office and would have been carried off were it not for Eichhorn, the revolutionary Berlin police chief and Independent SPD member, who intervened to have him released. The attempted kidnapping had been part of an assassination plot by a group of mercenaries hired by the Berlin military commandant, an SPD member. Their instructions were "to ferret out and hunt down [the leaders of the Spartacists] by day and by night to prevent them from carrying out either agitational or organisational work" (Frölich, p278). From then on Luxemburg and her comrades had to live as fugitives. She stayed in a different hotel every night under a false name, leaving early in the morning to avoid unwelcome visitors.

Groups of disgruntled soldiers returning from the front were being formed into paramilitary corps by the generals and whipped up into anti-revolutionary fervour. Gustav Noske of the SPD government was given the job of defence minister, and took supreme command of these forces — known as the Freikorps. They had every intention of marching into Berlin to smash the Communists and the revolution. But first they needed to lure them out onto the streets. On 4 January 1919 Eichhorn was sacked on trumped-up charges of embezzlement. This provoked outrage as he was seen as a man of the revolution and of integrity. A mass demonstration in support of Eichhorn took place on 5 January and the mood encouraged Liebknecht and the Revolutionary Shop Stewards to declare a Revolutionary Committee with the intention of taking power in Berlin.

This was a fateful mistake. Only a minority of workers were prepared to rise up – most still had illusions in bourgeois democracy – and the Communist programme specifically stated that a majority of workers must be won over in order to seize power. The decision was taken by Liebknecht without referring to the rest of the Communist Party. When Luxemburg heard of the action she rowed with Liebknecht, reproachfully saying, "Karl, is that our programme?" But once the rising was in motion, she couldn't desert it. She called for active, armed defence of the revolution – though she had no means to provide this. The Revolutionary Committee was not capable of giving a lead to the workers they had encouraged to take to the streets and occupy the buildings of Berlin. It dithered, considering negotiations with Ebert, while its supporters were holed up in buildings waiting for guidance.

On 11 January Ebert and Noske mobilised the Freikorps to take back Berlin by force. They unleashed slaughter and terror for the next three days, killing thousands of workers. The counter-revolution was on the offensive.

Luxemburg and other leaders of the Spartacists were advised to leave town for their own safety, but they refused. They could not abandon the workers in defeat. Finally the Freikorps dragged Luxemburg from her hiding place and murdered her along with Karl Liebknecht, throwing her body in the canal. "The old sow deserved no more," said Lieutenant Vogel, the officer in charge, displaying the Freikorps' hatred of everything Luxemburg represented (Dietmar Dath, *Rosa Luxemburg*, Suhrkamp, 2010, p7). Just before her death Luxemburg was able to write one last article. In "Order Reigns in Berlin", published in *Rote Fahne* on 14 January, she attempted to give workers an understanding of why the rising had failed, and how it could rise again:

"The leadership has failed. But the leadership can and must be re-created by the masses and out of the masses. The masses are the crucial factor; they are the rock on which the final victory of the revolution will be built... 'Order reigns in Berlin!' You stupid lackeys! Your order is built on sand. The revolution will 'raise itself up again clashing', and to your horror it will proclaim to the sound of trumpets: I was, I am, I shall be."

★ 17: LEGACY

The German Revolution did rise again, several times over the next four years, but the Communist Party, inexperienced and robbed of some of its finest leaders, was never able to give the lead necessary to overcome the ruling class. By the end of 1923 the revolutionary moment was over. The consequences of that failure could not have been graver. The Freikorps that had murdered Luxemburg went on to form the embryo of Hitler's street army. The Social Democrats who had set them loose went on to perish in the concentration camps under Hitler's reign. Luxemburg's ultimatum of socialism or barbarism was proved in the negative – the hope of socialism in Germany was crushed, but the forces unleashed to crush it could not be tamed, and the next two decades saw the greatest barbarism hitherto known to humanity.

The failure of the German Revolution also left the Russians stranded. By the late 1920s Stalin had taken over and strangled the nascent workers' state. Lenin had died in 1924 and was now treated as an idol – something that would have appalled him. Luxemburg was posthumously attacked for her arguments with him – she went from martyr to anti-Bolshevik enemy and her work was buried.

The New Left in the 1960s uncovered her again as a Marxist untainted by association with the Soviet Union, while dissidents in East Germany took inspiration from her. Feminists found in her a strong woman revolutionary and theorist — though some attacked her for not writing much on the woman question. Now there is a new resurgence of interest, with a steady stream of conferences, books and new collections of her writings.

Ours is a world Luxemburg would recognise: whole regions ravaged by imperialist war, deep pools of poverty in the global south, the working class being asked to pay for a crisis endemic to capitalism and reformist parties who only want to preserve the system. But we also are living in a new age of mass strikes — from Argentina, Bolivia and Venezuela in the early 2000s to Greece and Spain and the Arab Spring in 2011. Zetkin wrote of Luxemburg, "She was the sharp sword, the living flame of the revolution." The power of Rosa Luxemburg's writings and the example of her life burn as brightly today as they did a century ago.

FURTHER READING

Many of Luxemburg's key writings are available in various editions. *The Rosa Luxemburg Reader*, edited by Peter Hudis and Kevin B Anderson (Monthly Review Press, 2004), includes *The Mass Strike, Reform or Revolution, The Russian Revolution* and the *Junius Pamphlet* and extracts from *The Accumulation of Capital*, as well as her writings on women and more. *The Accumulation of Capital* is also available in complete form (Routledge, 2003). Verso is bringing out a *Collected Works* over the next decade. The first volume is *The Letters of Rosa Luxemburg* (Verso, 2011) and the next two will deal with her economic and political writings.

The classic biography is *Rosa Luxemburg* by Paul Frölich (Bookmarks, 1994). Peter Nettl's more detailed biography, *Rosa Luxemburg* (two volumes, Oxford, 1966), is out of print though can be tracked down in libraries or second hand. Tony Cliff helped to revive interest in Luxemburg on the British left with his *Rosa Luxemburg* (International Socialism, 1959). This is available on the Marxist Internet Archive, as are most of Luxemburg's writings: www.marxists.org

Those seeking an introduction to Marxist economics and the concept of accumulation could try Joseph Choonara's *Unravelling Capitalism* (Bookmarks, 2009). Judy Cox's review of *The Accumulation of Capital* provides a useful summary and critique: "Can capitalism go on forever?" in *International Socialism* 100 (Autumn 2003), pubs.socialistreviewindex.org.uk/isj100/cox.htm. On the German Revolution Chris Harman's *The Lost Revolution: Germany 1918-1923* (Bookmarks, 1997) and Pierre Broué's *The German Revolution* (Haymarket, 2006) are the best.